STOP WAITING TO BE GREAT

Ten Points To A Wealthy Start Now

Dr. Titus C. Wright

WRIGHT MEDIA GROUP, INC.
Philadelphia, PA

NOTES

NOTES

NOTES

Copyright 2019 Titus C. Wright

This publication may not be reproduced,
stored in a retrieval system or transmitted in
whole or in part, in any form or by any means
electronic, mechanical, photocopying, recording
or otherwise, without the prior written permission
of Wright Media Group Incorporated, First Edition 2019.
Copyright 2019 Wright Media Group Inc.
For information, Contact Special Sales Department
Wright Media Group, Inc. Philadelphia PA
(Email at: twrightmediagroup@gmail.com)

This Publisher and Author disclaim any personal liability, loss
or risk incurred as a consequence of the use and application,
either directly or indirectly, of any advice, information or
methods presented in this publication.
Printed in the United States of America

"The Blessing of the LORD, It Maketh RICH, and He Adds No Sorrow With It"
-Proverbs 10:22

NOTES

NOTES

A SIMPLE THOUGHT:

Are you still waiting to be great? After all those years of saying the same old tired thing, *"This is the year things will really start to happen!"* Time seems to go by very fast and you realize your dream of becoming a total success is slipping away. What are you doing to make your dream of becoming successful a reality? Once you finally realize that your future isn't in front of you or around you but it is inside of you, then things can begin to move. The things that can begin to move is your thinking. It is ultimately up to you to start this movement. What are you waiting for that needs to happen for you to become great/successful? Some people have simply just given up on greatness.

Most people really don't believe it could happen for them. They have simply just settled down on letting the wave carry them through life. What is your cut off point or shall I say, what is your cut off age? At what point will you give up on being great? Remember this saying, *"It's never too late to be what you should have been"-unknown.* When will you take some kind of action and start doing something toward your dream of becoming a winner? As I've heard motivational speakers say so many times, *"There is Greatness Within You!"* This book is designed to motivate you and hopefully give you a push in the right direction with ten important points to a wealthy start. It is to help you to get up and move toward a goal and not just sit there, Waiting To Be Great!

Starting your own business isn't an exact science. It is more of an art. Successful entrepreneurs are a very diverse group of people. You should seriously consider either becoming an entrepreneur or investor. In the long run, it would be to your best financial advantage. You can have the opportunity to be self empowered and really stake your claim, as they say, *"Put your dagger in the sand"*

It is true that nobody is going to come to your rescue when you are broke, busted, and disgusted. However, I do believe there are plenty of opportunities out there that will fit into your plan, if you have one. The key word here is *plan*. You've got to have a plan or strategy to get where you want to be. You need to start taking massive action and stop Waiting to Be Great.

Set yourself up for success where it should not depend on you being there. Make your business scalable. Your wealth cycle has to include Teamwork, Leadership, and Conditioning. All three have to be present in order for it to work. Try and get experts on your team. Don't be a "lone ranger". Don't try and do it all by yourself. Others will be compelled by your leadership to join you. Once you set up your structure and take action towards your vision, people will want to help. Communicate your vision clearly to make sure it is understood. Finding the best people for your wealth team is crucial for your success. I believe people who try to become *"self made"* always fail because they are missing a key ingredient, *"people"*. As they say, "The speed of the leader is the speed of the team". Be a team player by joining others in their wealth pursuits as well. You will come to understand that helping others helps *you*. Everything does come back, so take charge and lead your wealth. Focus your energies into productive tasks, not on unproductive busy activities. You need to recognize that everyone is in sales, even if they are not aware of it. Try and see where you can serve. What need can you meet or fulfill? Are you a product or service person or both? Either way, you've got to start with *people*. You could be an investor or entrepreneur. People need to be part of your equation if you want to become successful. Entrepreneurs know that their income is in direct proportion to their contribution in the market place.

THE MISSION IS NOT IMPOSSIBLE

My mission and vision for this book is to get you fired up about your financial future. If you have experienced failure time and time again then something needs fixing. It is possible to shake off failure and gravitate toward success. Some people only need a slight change in direction to find real and lasting success, while others may need a little more. You can become a victor instead of a victim by dropping that victim mentality. Business failure is devastating, however, you must understand that it is temporary and simply a part of the process of becoming successful. The bottom line here is to never give up and don't quit. As Donald Trump says, *"Never, ever give up! You can change and you can move around but never, ever give up!" (Trump 1997, Art of the Comeback).*

You need to make up your mind that being successful is a must and you have got to *do* it. Begin using words such as, *I Can, It is Possible, It's Not too Hard or Difficult for Me!* Let's be totally honest with ourselves by forgetting our ego, eliminating our pride, and being willing to get down to business *right now*. Let's try our best to focus on creating a product or service of value first and then offering it to others. Condition yourself for success. Experience a paradigm shift in habits.

Stallone reminds us that, *"It's not about how hard you get hit, but how much you can take and keep moving forward. That's how winning is done." -(2007, Rocky Balbao Film).*

You can apply these concepts right now when reading each of these points. Be patient, experience the difference and enjoy the process!

Chapter One

10 POINTS TOWARD A WEALTHY START:

"Everyone you meet in life is either an Example or a Warning" - Edward Mercer

Alice was a new business owner and doing exceptionally well. She was in her third year and was about to break even and start making a substantial profit. Alice was very excited to have survived the tough times and was looking forward to seeing her business rally take off.

One day Alice's friend Kate stopped by and told Alice her unfortunate story. Kate's story was so sad it made Alice cry. Kate had some troubling financial issues and needed help. Alice decided to help Kate. Alice knew she had financial obligations to her business, and employees, but she just couldn't see Kate go through her financial dilemma alone. Alice began to sacrifice her own responsibilities to help Kate. She took from here and there just to help her friend. She made decisions based on her emotions.

Soon Alice could not pay her own bills for the business. Alice tried to come up with money for the lease, phone, and supplies she desperately needed. She couldn't afford to keep her four employees. The business was in deep trouble and losing money fast. Overall, Alice had no emergency funds to sustain her operation. There were unexpected cancellations from a few key clients that Alice depended on. Alice had to sell her car and other personal items to try and save her business, but it was too late. The business failed. Before long, Alice had a sadder story than Kate.

Point #1: Develop A Better Relationship With Money.

What is your relationship with money? Is it a good one or is it bad? If It is good, then you are okay but if it is bad, then you won't be successful until this is fixed. First things first. I want to help you in repairing your relationship with money to put things in order. What happened? Have you had a falling out, big fight or argument with your money in the past? Did money leave you because of a misunderstanding? Let's just pretend that money is a person, more like a phenomenal employee that works for you. You have to recognize that you are the boss over money. You are in charge of it. Howbeit, you need to be a good boss because money should work for you, not you for money. Money is your subordinate. I heard someone say, *"Money makes a good servant but a bad master."*

Although money is your best servant, you still have to respect it or it will go away. Yes, lets pretend that money is a person you really care about and like very much. You enjoy the friendship you have with money and want to keep things on a professional/platonic basis. You don't want to fall in love with it, cross the line, or get personal with it. This would lead to creating a hostile environment. Let money know that you like it, but you're not in love with it. If you fall in love with money, somebody is going to get hurt. You should never lie, cheat, or do anything untoward involving money. It would be a very bad situation and your good relationship with money would become strained. Trust would be destroyed.

Does your money respect you? If it doesn't, then you need to stop mistreating and betraying it. What do I mean by saying all this? I'm talking about your loyalty. You may say, you really like money and would like to have more. So why when you get it, you are so eager to get rid of it. You're always so eager to trade it away for stuff. They call it *spending*. Money will not stand for this kind of behavior for too long. When money realizes that you actually like the things it can buy better, eventually, money will go away. It will leave you! So, let's patch up your attitude and behavior towards money, so you can move on and start accumulating. If you are ready to rekindle a healthy relationship with money it would be a win/win situation for you. If you treat money right, it will treat you right, and you will have more of it.

Money loves the words compounded interest and growth and you should too. In his book, *Money: Master the Game*, Tony Robbins discusses in detail *Asset Allocation* and *Compounding*. It's probably one of his obsessions. After all he is a very wealthy man. Money is always looking for a good place to stay and just chill. Give money a good home. Financial guru Suze Orman also tells us to put our money in a Money Market IRA, such as a 401k, 403(b) or other Roth account. A money market account is also a good holding place for new potential investors until they decide where to invest their money later. Compound growth works like magic.

Suze teaches that the growth potential in a 401K retirement plan is better than just sticking it into a regular retirement account. This is pre taxed savings. An employee sponsored 401k is good because some employers do match a certain percentage of the funds that you decide to put into it. Who is going to argue with free money? I also know personally that stock can be a good investment too, if you don't panic when the market dips a little. Remember, you only lose money when you sell in a panic. You've got to exercise some patience. When I was in my late twenties *(a hundred years ago!)* I lost my job. I sold my stock and was able to live for an entire year without having to work. I had plenty of money to survive on until I got another job. Even though investing in stock is riskier than real-estate, it can be liquidated faster. If I had been waiting to sell a piece of property, I would have starved to death. Financial advisor and author David Bock also mentions that a SEP IRA account is the perfect product for the self employed. He says that even if the entrepreneur files bankruptcy or just fails in business after ten years those funds are government protected. So all is not lost if the business ends. As the business owner you may be eligible for a tax credit up to $500 each year for the first three years (A Merrill Edge® Small Business). It is one of the ideal ways to have a retirement fund if you are self employed.

I also like the idea of having an emergency fund unlike our opening example in Alice's case. If you have any kind of job, then you should be able to save something out of each check. George Clason's book, *The Richest Man in Babylon,* literally changed my life forever. There is a statement that put me on the road to financial freedom. It says, *"Part of what I earn, I get to keep."* This sounds very simplistic, but it made a giant impact on me. When I read it, I realized that no one gets to handle my money before I do (except the IRS). So, that means I'm the one who decides who gets paid first, and I choose me! This is in line with the *pay yourself first,* school of thought. Within a two week period, I was able to open 5 bank accounts with a clear financial plan in mind. For so many people, *being broke* tends to sneak up on them without notice. My accounts get paid first because they are part of my financial security plan. I always allocate a portion of my income to those first. It doesn't have to be a large amount initially, but make sure you're saving something from every pay check and be consistent. Let some bills wait and do this first.

One of those five accounts represent an emergency fund money market account. I believe having a cushion of at least six to eight months of savings for emergency living expenses (just in case you find yourself without a job) is a wise decision. This should be set up with automatic deductions from your paycheck.

Do you realize how long it takes to find another job if you are suddenly laid off today? It doesn't matter how many college degrees you have. It could take up to a year. Trust me on this one, I've been there more than once. You should really start putting your money to work because money enjoys working. Give your money a job to do and begin looking at your money differently. Start seeing your money as a friendly person and not a menacing foe. Make it a habit to smile when you get bills in the mail. Anger and bills are a bad combination to associate with money. You don't want to start scaring money away with your bad attitude. Remember, we are still working on rebuilding your relationship with money.

Proverbs state, *"Labor not to be rich..."*[2].

If you focus on a higher purpose, the money will take care of itself. You should be working with passion and true purpose. Don't do things for money, but focus on being successful and being grateful.

Point #2: Being Broke Is Very Abnormal.

If you are broke, it is definitely not normal. It is unnatural and incongruent with what we see daily when we go outside. If you are broke, then something is very wrong. Look up in the sky and see that air is plentiful. You are not going to breath all of that fresh air in one day, even in an entire lifetime, yet there is an abundance. There is plenty of sky, water, trees, rocks, dirt, sand and just about every natural resource in Gods great world. As David in the old testament said, *"My cup runs over."*[3] The universe is unlimited and so are its resources. The question here is, with all of this abundance at your availability, why aren't you rich?

Wild animals are not poor? They don't even have a job! They don't worry about paying bills, rent/mortgage, or driving the latest sports car, yet they eat, sleep and function very well. They know that there is an abundance of everything they need. If a polar bear wanted fresh fish, shrimp, salmon, lobster, or even caviar (rotten fish eggs), he isn't going to the nearest seafood store to buy it. He goes to the abundant stream, open 24/7 and gets as much as he wants for free. Why is it that humans are the only living species that has to pay to live? The only limitations you have are the ones you decide to accept. I will go as far in saying that poverty is a sin and a curse. Just as wealth is the result of success, poverty is a result of some kind of failure. Both are the result of your thinking. Poverty is a state of mind and so is wealth. There can be no compromise between poverty and riches as they both move in opposite directions. If you change your negative thoughts, you'll change your circumstance. Poverty is out of line with nature.

Put it in your mind to shake off poverty and what you lack because its unnatural. Poverty has always been used as a curse in the bible, *"Cursed shall be thy basket and thy store"*[4]. See! This proves that being broke is not the norm, even in God's eyes. It is similar to being sick which is not normal either. If sickness was the norm, why do we so eagerly go to the hospital, or seek doctors to get well? We need to be financially healthy too. If being poor was normal, God would not have used it in the old testament to pass judgments such as famine and lack on nations as a punishment. I don't think that God is punishing you. Your negative thinking is punishing you. In the Bible, when God judged nations for disobedience, He caused a disruption in the natural flow of abundance. Prosperity is always flowing in the Earth, only a divine intervention from God could interrupt it. It is very natural for the land to be extremely rich and yield its abundance. It's all part of nature's ecosystem. To be rich is normal and in balance with nature.

Why are so many people comfortable with being broke? We live in an abundant world. There are no shortages anywhere. There is only abundance everywhere. This is what you have to see for yourself. Open your eyes and look around you. What do you need for yourself? If you say *"I need a car, house, money or whatever,"* you need to already see yourself as having these things. They are all visibly noticeable around you every day. When I look down the street, I see tons of cars, houses, and people with jobs working everywhere. You just have to do as the Bible instructs, *"Believe that you have these things and you shall have them."* Again, being rich is more natural than being poor.

You need to begin to set a higher standard for yourself today. Prepare your mind to jump into the flow of abundance. If you were about to jump into a stream, it won't stop moving and wait until you get in. You'll just have to jump into the flow and such is life. The ocean is not like a bus that stops and waits for you to hop on. It never stops moving. It flows 24 hours a day and 7 days a week. Thus, success is not in short supply it's like an ocean. As Jim Rohn said in his Youtube 2007 motivational speech, *"Some people go to the ocean with a teaspoon. They should trade it in for a bucket. They'll look better down at the ocean, and kids won't make fun of them."* I truly believe that the only limits people have are the ones they place on themselves. I have a good friend who is totally blind, yet he runs a television network and several restaurants. He truly has vision. He is a millionaire. In his younger years as a blind person, people had often suggested that he get a box and beg on the streets. He refused and rejected the idea because he knew of the greatness within himself.

God is about abundance and extravagance. The only way to get beyond scarcity is to start beyond it. Get rid of your poverty consciousness and put your mind in an abundant state. How is this done? You need to start being more generous in small ways. Give a tithe (10 percent) from your earnings. I used to figure out how to pay God ten percent after paying all my bills. Then I realized that I should pay God first and then figure out how to pay my bills. All of my bills miraculously got paid. The money started showing up unrepentantly. If you have a dollar then give a dime. This will get your mind out of the lack mentality. We live in a very rich world. Jesus said, *"Open your eyes and look on the field, the harvest is plentiful but the laborers are few"*[5]. Yes, there is work for you to do. Stop saying I want or I need. This reinforces to your subconscious that you are in lack. Thus lack attracts more lack. You have to develop a rich consciousness. Stop complaining about what you don't have and expect abundance everyday. Start thanking God for whatever you want as though you already have it. Believe me, He never disappoints. I do this all of the time. I'm already thanking God for helping me sell 30 million copies of this book. Visualize and speak abundance and it will show up. Also, change your physiology and start looking and feeling successful.

Point 3: Be Wise With Your Resources.

When you are in business as a start-up, be very careful with your spending or lending out funds, especially if you are still struggling. You really cannot effectively help anyone financially until you can help yourself. Put yourself in a solid position before you are able to strengthen others. Strengthen yourself first. During an airplane drill, instructions are given to, *Put On Your Own Oxygen Mask First,* before you try to assist a child or others. Jesus told Peter to *"First strengthen yourself, then strengthen your brethren"*

Don't forget the order of things. There will be some people you may be able to help just a little, it all depends upon where you are financially. I'm not talking about being down right stingy. Giving is a healthy part of life, but you need to use wisdom with it. This area will be discussed in more detail later. There is another quote I heard years ago in a seminar it says, *"If your outgo exceeds your income, then your upkeep will be your downfall."* You know what you can do without hurting yourself or jeopardizing your own success. As they say when it comes to life and business, it's all about the details. Watch those resources because they are your seeds to prosperity.

Point 4: Success Is Not a Secret. It Is an Attitude.

Having a bad attitude toward success has ruined lots of people. To actually look at yourself and think that you have finally made it, you begin to rest on your laurels and is the beginning of the end. Things are constantly changing, especially in today's advanced technological world. You could be up today and down tomorrow, just that quickly. Many successful entrepreneurs will tell you to never take your eyes off the ball. You have to stay totally focused. One thing billionaire investor Warren Buffet says is to always act as if someone is gaining on you. He says to never be at rest when it comes to business. I believe that you should never stop learning and growing. Maintaining is okay, but you have to continue to grow. As long as you are moving forward and making progress you are growing and feel you are accomplishing something. Progress is forward motion. Some people say that success is a law, science, or system, howbeit, it is not a secret. Les Brown says in his 1994 book, *Live Your Dreams*, *"People are waiting for their ship to come in but people who win in life are willing to swim out to meet it."*

I truly believe that the best investment you can make is in yourself, your own learning and self development. As a university professor, I've got to keep studying and learning new things to be able to share with my students. I read at least 5 books a month. I can't afford to rest on my laurels of past successes. I will always be a student of learning first and a teacher second. This attitude keeps me humble and levelheaded. The more I learn, the more I realize how much I need to learn. I am so grateful for the opportunity to teach others.

Attitude changes our perspective. There is nothing worse than having a job that you've *"Got to do"*, as opposed to having one you *"Get to do"*. If a change in attitude is gratefulness then our perspective changes. Learn to be grateful and appreciative. I believe that the minute you learn to be grateful, you become rich. It is true that you should be rich but God owes you nothing. If someone gives you a gift, you need to say thank you. The Earth's abundance is a gift to us all. Arrogance is a dream killer. You need to be humble and grateful. The Bible states that *"God resists the proud but gives grace to the humble."*[7] Don't let success go to your head. keep your feet on the ground.

Joshua 1:8 states- *"This book of the law shall not depart out of thy mouth; but thou shall meditate therein day and night, that thou may observe to do according to all that is written therein: for then thou shall make thy way prosperous, and then thou shall have good success"*[8] True Success comes with a change of attitude.

Point 5: See The Value In What You Already Have.

In the book of Genesis, the oldest son of Isaac, whose name was Esau, sold his birthright to his younger brother Jacob for a lousy plate of food. A birthright in those days meant having an entitlement or being the first heir of an inheritance. It was extremely valuable. Either Esau did not realize the value of his birthright or just didn't care.

Esau seemed to have had a legitimate need; he was hungry and wanted food. His brother Jacob had just made a big pot of delicious stew. The irony here is that Esau was a very good cook of which his father loved the venison he would often prepare for him. Esau was probably just lazy that day. Jacob was not known for his culinary skills but he was very crafty and surreptitious.

When Esau made the foolish deal with his brother of trading his birthright for some stew, it was a permanent decision based on a temporary situation. All of a sudden a bowl of stew became more important and more valuable to him. Later,

Esau regretted his bad decision and realized the importance of his birthright, but it was too late to reverse his decision. The deal was done. How many blessings have you tossed away for what seemed to be legitimate reasons and later realized you'd made a big mistake based on a moment of temporary discomfort?

Some blessings are inherited, so the value may not always be quickly appreciated. We need to see the value in what we have been given. As a child, my father's favorite saying was, *"Use what you've got to make what you want."* He was a very resourceful man. I heard it said, *"It's not always about your resources, but it's about your resourcefulness."* Don't give up and throw in the towel when you face hardships. As top motivational speaker Dr Eric Thomas says, *"Pain is temporary. It may last for a day, month, or even a year, but eventually it will subside. If I quit and give up however, it will last forever."* He went on to say, *"It's okay to cry but don't cry to quit. Cry to keep going!"* -*(2015 Speech, Michigan State university)*

At times we all get frustrated and are tempted to make unwise decisions. I have a younger brother who is a borderline genius. A few years ago, he played chess around the country. He was a whiz kid in the game, however, when he made an obvious bad chess move he would get very angry and frustrated. He often got so upset with himself that he would end up sabotaging the entire game. Don't sabotage your success!

The world has an old saying, *"Whomever the gods seek to destroy, they first made mad."* Sometimes in life, we get worried and frustrated about things. We get upset and angry when things don't fall into place according to our expectations. Don't let the things that happen in your business or personal life cause you to make bad decisions. There is hope. Hang in there, and you can make it. *"Never ask what did I do wrong.*

Ask what did I do right?"- Brian Tracy.

In the past, I was able to overcome many challenges in my business because I was able tobe alone and think. I was open to hearing instruction from that inner voice. I call God. You should never focus on the problem but rather focus on finding a solution. Every other motivational guru will tell you that, *"whatever you focus on, you get more of."* This means that if you focus on success, then success will come. However, if you focus on your failures, then more of that will occur. It's part of the laws of attraction. Never discard your assets out of fear and doubt. There are people out there just waiting for you to become desperate enough to sell your prized possessions.

During the recession and real-estate crash in the mid to late 2000's, there were a few people still making big money while everyone else was losing it. They made money because they were busy capitalizing on other people's fears. Many wise investors were buying real-estate at extremely low prices. I'm sure you've heard the saying, *"One mans trash is another man's treasure."* They were doing the opposite or as they say, going against the grain of what others were doing. These investors knew that this was not the end, and the market would recover as it always have. They knew the crash was a temporary situation. When the market eventually recovered, these unorthodox investors became multimillionaires several times over. They saw value where others could not.

During the Dot-com era of the late 80's, everybody was jumping on board this *new* seemingly *lucrative* opportunity. They couldn't understand why Warren Buffet wasn't excited and jumping on the Dot-Com wagon too. Some people even criticized him and thought he was out of touch for not investing in such a seemingly promising opportunity. Eventually, when the Dot-com bubble burst, everybody lost their shirts, except Warren. We should never be too quick to adapt to other people's pessimism or even their optimism. As we learned earlier, *you've got to follow your gut/instincts.* Successful entrepreneurs tend to swim against the current.

Buffet didn't become one of the top three richest man in the world by being stupid. He says he only invests in businesses he understands.
In a 2013 an internet interviewer asked Buffet, if given the opportunity to own all of the gold in the world, or an equal value of farm land, which would he choose? He picked the farmland. Warren says, a block of gold would just sit there looking pretty and do nothing. It would not produce anything of itself, if the stock didn't go up. He says buying farmland however, would be a better investment because it would have usage potential. If the value of the stock didn't increase, at least he could grow fruit and vegetables on the land and sell the produce multiple times over.

Some investors pride themselves in buying merchandise only when the owner absolutely, desperately has to sell. Then they know they can get it dirt cheap. Remember, stay confident, be calm, and don't panic when facing hard times. Get alone by yourself and meditate for a few minutes. Center yourself and develop the habit of listening. You don't want to get distracted but be totally focused. Again, *You can't take your eyes off the ball!*

Point 6: Stay Cool, Calm and Collected.

When it comes to acquiring things in life, as they say, you should never let them see you sweat! This is not just good advice in the business world, but in everyday life too. I believe in hard work as long as it is smart and effective. You should never think that you need to push, shove or start doing questionable activities in order to get ahead. Tony Robbins says in his 2014 block buster book, Money Master the game, *"Riches are what you have, while wealth is what you have become"*

I truly believe that the process of becoming wealthy is just as important as achieving it. Make sure the end justifies your ethical means. Most successful people would agree that, to be a winner, you have to think like a winner.

I believe whatever God has for you, is for you. This thinking neutralizes a lot of stress. I am not giving you a license to be lazy. Some people often have a habit of saying, *"Let God do it."* and they sit back and do nothing. Faith in itself is okay but you've got to get up and do something. You've got to get physically moving and get it done. The Bible states that *"Faith without works is dead."*9 You've got to do the work.

As Les Brown says, *"No one can write your book, no one can dream your dream, and no one can tell your story better than you can."* You should learn to position yourself for success. Be aware of how you can start putting yourself in the right places at the right time. The world needs your ideas and your input. Success is always waiting for an opportunist to show up. Success is the key to everything. Focus on it first.

Don't forget that the process is extremely important. If there is a lot of heartache and pain in trying to get a deal done, then step back and regroup. Don't be desperate, keep your cool. People often say, *don't sweat the small stuff.* Guess what? It's all small stuff. Don't be afraid to be willing to walk away. If the deal is meant for you to have, it will come back. You need to learn to just settle down and ask God for guidance. A short prayer will center you.

I can honestly and truly say that every major milestone and blessing in my life was not difficult to accomplish. I look back now and realize that I was never out of breath trying to acquire things I really wanted. When I purchased my beautiful home, it was one of the easiest transactions I had ever done. My wife and I looked at the house in February and went to closing in March (a month later). When I decided to go back to school, it was not a difficult task. Even though it took me seven plus years to complete four separate degrees, I managed to finish top in my class throughout the entire process. I still can't believe how simple it was to accomplish but God was in it. I did work very hard and the process added so much value to my life..

We do have to be diligent as well as vigilant in life & business when opportunities avail themselves. I do believe that in order to succeed, you have to take effective massive action. This action does not have to be hurtful, harmful, or stressful. You should be willing to do what is required but not with sorrow of heart. Another passage in the book of Proverbs states, *"The blessing of the Lord makes rich, and adds no sorrow with it."* True wealth should always attracted and never pursued.

When the Apple corporation produces a new I-Phone, customers wait in line, days at a time in order to be the first to purchase that very high end product. The price ranges between $700-$1000 per phone. The Apple stores never have to run after customers when these phones go on sale at midnight (in most cases).

Even though being successful does take work, the tasks are not grueling if God is in it. The Bible does say, *"My yolk is easy, and my burden is light."*[11] This book is not about religion, but I believe that you can expand financially by expanding spiritually. Start being grateful for where you are now. *Gratitude* is the real secret that unlocks the door to wealth. This is where real success derives.

Point 7: Spend Less Than You Earn.

This point sounds so superfluous and just common sense. In all of my many years of experience and learning, there is one major thing that I've come to realize and that is, *common sense ain't all that common.*

Most people would agree that wealth is not limited to just money. You could have a wealth of knowledge, ideas, influence, power, expertise, etc. Most people, when starting out in business have very little working capital with nothing to waste. It is intrinsic that every dollar you spend is seen as an investment in your business or your personal development. Let your investments be a round trip ticket that will eventually return back to you, never a one way trip. If you have a job and are someday seeking to invest, then you have got to spend less than you earn and invest the difference. As said earlier, put the extra money in a money marker account until you decide where to invest it. An investment that does not result in additional increase could result in a potential loss. Forget trying to look like a big shot. You're not! I heard a friend say that his definition of a big shot is *a little shot that kept on shooting* (I thought that was funny).

There are assets and liabilities and you need to know the difference between them. Assets make you money and liabilities cost you money. Anything that does not increase your income is a liability. Poor people buy liabilities, wealthy people buy assets. If you have a business, you should not purchase anything that does not result in some kind of a return. This goes for advertising, marketing, equipment, and anything you spend money on. Advertising guru, David Ogilvy made sure that his client's money and efforts was never wasted on slick, entertaining yet ineffective advertising. He is known for saying, *"Test, test, and test some more. Test your advertising, marketing, product, or service, and never stop testing."* This was his measuring system for progress and making sure his clients were getting a return on their advertising dollars. (1983 Ogilvy on Advertising).

Trial and error are okay if money isn't an issue. In most cases money is a concern, especially when you're first starting up a new venture. This is serious business. You need to create a budget and stick to it, no matter what! Before you spend a dime always second-guess yourself before you make a move. I'm not saying become paranoid, but try to spend your money wisely and never be in a hurry to purchase anything! If you miss a so-called bargain, so what! You can't lose what you've never had. Don't buy anything on credit. If you can't pay for it in cash, you don't need it! Simply operate slightly below your means. Watch those dollars!

You Must Sell Something to Get Rich! If you want to make some money, let's face it, you've got to have something to sell. Here are the real questions you should be trying to answer: What do you have to sell? What do you want to sell? Are you good at tangible or intangible product selling? Tangible represents a physical product such as a book, equipment, food, or anything a person gets to physically own. Intangible represents a service, idea, a system a solution or concept such as insurance, education, any service oriented transaction. Even though this book is tangible it mostly represent the intangible. The most important value in purchasing this book is not the paper but the information it holds. Therefore it is basically an intangible service product. I am selling wisdom and knowledge with this book.

The next battery of questions are: Who do you want to sell to? How do you plan on selling it? Where will you sell it? When are you planning on selling it? And why do you want to sell this particular product or service anyway? Bottom line here is, whatever you do decide to sell, make sure you truly believe in what you are selling. You have to be explosively excited and convinced that what you are selling is definitely something you would use yourself. Is it something people really need or want? It has to be something that will add a true benefit to those who purchase it. Even if you decided to open up a street car wash, make sure you are giving the best possible service ever. Give great value and benefit. A little kindness and respect to all customers goes a long way too. Give customers the king or queen treatment. Make them feel good about stopping and getting their car washed at your location. Make sure you do an exceptional job so they would want to come back again and again. Remember, you are not just making a sale, you are making a customer. You should be thinking long term relationship with every customer that patronizes your business. As it is said, you only get one chance to make a first impression, so make it a good one!

      This same formula can be applied to any kind of business. This includes a dental practice, doctors office, law firm, insurance agency, retail store, boutique, barber shop/hair salon, accounting firm and any business involving the public. You must believe and have passion for what you are selling and others will catch your enthusiasm. Make sure you are doing something that you truly enjoy. The good feelings of your enjoyment will resonate to every customer. People DO want to feel good when they are purchasing something. As I heard someone once say, *"Sell the sizzle, not just the steak."* Selling something is the only way for you to get rich. I recommend that you learn how to sell and find a product or service that you believe in and that fits your personality. Purchase books on selling and selling techniques. The better you get at it, the more money you will make. Selling anything is easy if you are convinced that it will make a difference in people's lives. Look at it as you are helping people and doing them a favor.

Point 8: Have Passion, Love What You Do.

Bottom line, if you don't absolutely love what you do, then stop doing it. If you don't love it, you will eventually quit when the tough times come. When you love what you do, you'll work harder. As a matter of fact it isn't really work to you. If you are saying that, "I don't know what I really love to do yet", this means the world is open to your own imagination. You've got to get out there and see what you're attracted to. You've got to involve yourself in lots of things until something clicks for you.

I became involved in radio broadcasting by accident when a friend asked me to drive him to the radio station. When we went inside, I soon realized that radio was what I really loved and wanted to do. I was actually good at it. Eventually I got into television, produced a music video, published magazines, and stated writing books. I guess I fell in love with communications.

When you discover what it is that you love, then you need to find a niche to serve. Find a specific market for your particular product or service. You may be saying, "I have a lot of interests. I want to do everything." Let me make this easier for you. It's called focus. Pick one of your talents, or skills and perfect it. You don't want to be a "jack of all trades and a master of none". You've got to be focused. In his 2004 book Reallionaire, Dr. Pharrah Gray says, *"Find something that you can do so well that nobody can do it just like you. Love it so much, that you would do it for free."* Sometimes you just have to get your foot in the door. The work that I now do, I would actually do it for free. (I'm glad they pay me for it though!).

If you want to start a business, it may start small with little revenue, however it may have great potential. Work with all of your strength, be diligent and experience the blessing. I heard someone say, *"It will work if you work it!"* Don't worry if your friends laugh at you, just keep at it. Double down on that which is working and eliminate that which is not. Before long, you will be the one laughing all the way to the bank. Go into an area that has a large potential profit margin. However, money should not be your main reason for getting into a business. Your passion and desire to serve others should be your true motivation. *"Without passion you don't have energy. Without energy you have nothing"*- Trump.

Whatever you have, be it product, service, or concept, sell it with passion and purpose. Have a true mission and purpose. If you have a viable mission, energy will be present. Be first class with it and present it from your heart. You can persuade, inspire, and influence customers, without using manipulation. *"If what you are offering is good, people will tell others. They will shout about it."* -Jeff Bezos– Amazon founder.

Point 9: Be A Go-Giver and Not A Go-Getter or Taker.

There is nothing wrong with developing a win/win relationship with a customer. No one has to be the loser in any of your business transactions. Society tells us that someone has to lose. In his book, *The Seven Habits of Highly Effective People,* Steven Covey reminds us that a win/win situation can be achieved. Covey says that you have to *"Begin with the end in mind and know how you want your meeting or presentation to go."* In essence he is saying to *see the end in the very beginning".*

Be prepared to add value to the customer. Don't have a taker mentality. You need to have the mind set of giving first and asking second. Create something of true value first, then offer it to potential customers. Show up with service to the customer in mind and begin to think about what the customer needs and wants. A good rule would be to under promise and over deliver. There are some people that will tell you to go through the door without the answer and when you get under pressure, you'll discover the answer. I don't believe in jumping out of a window and learning to fly on the way down. That's called suicide. I like being prepared because it helps build confidence. I believe as an entrepreneur that you should always give customers more than they expect. It needs to be about the customer first. Think of how you can serve them better. Listening is also the key. Remember, sales is like a ping pong game. There has to be even exchange, thus win/win. Sell with passion and integrity. Begin to think outside of yourself. Put yourself in the shoes of the customer. Business should capture a customers heart, not just their pocket book. Think of winning a customer, not just a sale. Know that you must give value to receive value. Always build your business based on telling the truth. Try and give more value for what you are paid. Give customers the *wow factor* in service. Giving more even works on a job. Try to wow your boss. *"Anything that won't sell, I don't want to invent" -Thomas Edison.* Make sure you have something you would want to use yourself.

Demand integrity from yourself. Learn to put everything you've got into anything you do. Don't think you need to save something for later. Believe me, later will have another set of benefits and values you can offer to new customers.

Point 10: True Wealth is Attracted, Never Pursued.

There is a way of drawing opportunities and prosperity to you. No, I'm not talking about theoretic laws of attracting things, but a real life practical application. You can zero in on the kinds of people that may be interested in buying your product, service or concept. Being all things to all people is not a good practical strategy. There needs to be a specific niche or group of people for what you are offering. If I were selling surf boards, then my niche would be surfers and beach goers.

Once you have established this niche, then you can create a solid strategy for attracting these kinds of people to your offering. Think of what you can give to them first. Use the *AIDA* approach which is interpreted as getting the customer's: *Attention, Interest, Desire (*for your product or service), and *Action,* (closing the deal). How do we get a potential customer to act? Give something of value to them first. I was very successful in selling radio advertising on my local radio station because I would produce a commercial for that business, unsolicited. I would go to that business and let them hear it. Many times once they heard it, they'd be impressed and would want to advertise. They would ask where can they advertise it. I then proceeded to tell them that I had a radio station in the neighborhood. I made sure the commercials were excellently produced.

Author Dr. Victor Frankl says in his best selling book, **Man's Search for Meaning,** *"For success, like happiness cannot be pursued; it must ensue, and it does so as the unintended side-effect of ones dedication to a cause greater than oneself..."*
Success has to be the result of your servitude. As author Grant Cardone says in his ground breaking NY Times best selling book, **The 10 X Rule**, *"Success isn't what happens to you, it's* ***because of you.*** *"* If you focus on adding so much value to others, you can't help but to get paid for it. I realize that people hate to be sold things but they love to buy. Your job is to help them buy. No one wants to feel as though they have been customarily sold something or manipulated. This is why you

should sell with passion and inspiration. Learn to inspire people to buy from you. Give them an intrinsic reason to purchase your product or service. Be exciting and upbeat. You need to be excited about what you are selling because people feed off on your excitement. If you are not sold on your own product or service, others won't be sold on it either. It is easier to get people to feel the way you feel than to get them to think the way your think. Your emotions are contagious. If you don't believe me, just go somewhere and start yawning. You will have lots of copycats.

When you sell using inspiration, good feelings, and passion, they will buy from you without buyers remorse. People love feeling good about their decisions. You are actually selling good feeling centered around your product or service. What can you give of value first to attract customers? You will be entering the law of cause and affect. Whatever you send out comes back. I hope you got the point!

NOTES

NOTES

NOTES

"Do what you can as well as you can do it, even if it is something you don't like"
-Bob Proctor

"Simplicity is the highest form of sophistication"
-Leonardo Da Vinci

"Some say, if I had more money I would have a better plan, but it should be, If I had a better plan, I would have more money"
-Brian Tracy

"If your ship doesn't come in, Swim out to meet it"
-Les Brown

"How you do anything, is how you do everything"
-Jack Canfield

"Massive action creates massive results"
-Grant Cardone

"Imagination and knowledge is the key to becoming successful"
-Donald J. Trump

CONCLUSION OF THE WHOLE MATTER:

"Those that can see the invisible can do the impossible".
- Tyrese

Congratulations! By now, you should be seeing changes in your life. Some people believe that the amount of money a person makes is important. I believe what you do with whatever money you have is more important. However, doing what you really love while meeting a need and serving others is the *Key* to fulfillment. This is extremely important! These practical concepts are just the beginning.

This book's subtitle does mention *Wealth, Success,* and *Prosperity*. These three appear to be the same, however, they are not. Wealth is moving forward with no particular state of emotion. It could be summed up as cash flow. Success is an internal feeling or state of being. It is a state of mind derived from fulfillment. Prosperity is the combination of them both being in balance and congruent with each other. It is possible to be wealthy without feeling successful. Success gives wealth meaning. Inherited wealth needs meaning attached to it. This is why so many wealthy people become philanthropists, give to charities or start foundations. Now that you have completed this reading, use the information in this book as a reference. Refer to it often. Keep it close to you for continued guidance toward making wise decisions for Achieving Success, Wealth and Prosperity in Life & Business.

Congratulations and continued SUCCESS!

ABOUT THE AUTHOR
Dr. Titus C. Wright

Titus Wright the CEO of Wright Media Group and the inspired author of *How To Get The Man/Woman of Your Dreams*. Dr. Titus motivates thousands of people per week with his *Positive Force* Youtube videos, magazine publications, and self help books.

Titus was blessed to have earned two Masters degrees in business administration/management. He also received a (Ph.D.) Doctorate of Philosophy in Christian Education. He shares his views and practical business strategies as a motivational speaker and university professor. Titus has dedicated his life to personal self development and in helping others find their true purpose and passion.

He has appeared on local and national television shows, numerous radio programs and in newsprint/magazines. Titus lives in Pennsylvania with his lovely wife, Coral.

STOP WAITING TO BE GREAT is Titus's fourth nationwide book release. This book is considered by far, one of the most revealing, straight forward and helpful to date. It is said by many that his books are worth their weight in *Pure Gold*. His multimedia organization continues to thrive due to these God-given points, rules and steps. He adheres to his own advice and has been able to implement these concepts in his own life and business. Titus believes that, prosperity isn't about owning things. It's about nothing owning you!

Contact email: twrightmediagroup@gmail.com
Available for corporate and academic speaking engagements.

Other Books By Dr. Titus C. Wright

Get Your Copy Today! One of a Kind Books From
The #1 Motivated Author: Dr. Titus C. Wright

AMAZON.COM/TITUS C. WRIGHT

Business Success
ALL NEW! TITLES!

Relationship Success
How To Get The Woman Of Your Dreams
& Man of Your Dreams

Two, One of a Kind Books That Every Person Should Have In Their Personal Collection

NOTES

NOTES

www.ingramcontent.com/pod-product-compliance
Lightning Source LLC
Chambersburg PA
CBHW050304220526
45465CB00002B/820